Footsteps of the past

William Booth

The troublesome teenager who changed the lives of people no-one else would touch

ANDREW EDWARDS AND FLEUR THORNTON

●••••• SEE TRAVEL WITH

good start

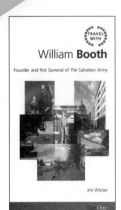

TRAVEL WITH
William **Booth**

Founder and first General of The Salvation Army

Jim Winter

Day One

LOOK OUT FOR THIS!
Throughout the book you
will see this at the top of
each page. If you have a
copy of *Travel with William
Booth* it will help you to
explore the story of Booth in
more detail—
but it is not essential.

*Travel with Wiliam Booth is
available from
Day One Publications.*

DayOne

Meet William Booth

There was always a side to Billy that wanted to go against the authorities of the day. With a deep faith in what he believed and a desperate wish to change life for the needy people around him, Billy became one of the best known people of his time who started a charity that is still going strong today.

Question 1

How could one troublesome boy influence so many people in the world?

Question 2

What have elephants, camels and boxers got to do with The Salvation Army?

Question 3

How can it be right to upset so many people by doing what you believe in?

Question 4

Is there any more to The Salvation Army than brass bands playing carols at Christmas?

Read on to find the answers...

❖•••••• SEE **TRAVEL WITH WILLIAM BOOTH** PAGES 23–26

A good start to life?

The execution took place at 8 o'clock in the morning. Minutes later the body was hanging limply from the gallows. William Saville, who was a twenty-nine year old farm labourer, had brutally murdered his wife and three children. People from the area had gathered to witness the punishment being carried out. In fact, so many people came, that the crush became deadly. People pushed and panicked. Seventeen ended up dead and hundreds were seriously injured.

Murders, highway robberies, mysterious stabbings of women in the streets at night, crimes of every kind, public executions and public whippings—witnessed by enormous crowds of people—escapes from the county jail and riots! Into this world was born our hero—William Booth.

William was born in Sneinton, Nottingham on 10 April 1829. King George IV was on the throne. William's father, Samuel, was a successful builder whose motto to his young son was 'Make money—and plenty of it!' William's mother, Mary, was a farmer's daughter. The family lived in a large, six bedroom house in the suburbs of Nottingham. William's eldest brother, Henry, had died when he was only three, but then came Ann who was his older sister. Younger than William were his sisters Emma and Mary.

The area around where they lived had been described as '…a sunny suburb with plenty of flowers and bright meadows, with the sparkling River Trent running through its valleys.' William enjoyed a lot of his childhood wandering along the banks of the River Trent, either reading or fishing in its waters. It all sounds ideal but the things happening around were worrying the young William.

FACT BOX:
William Booth was just eight years old when Queen Victoria came to the throne in 1837. She died at 81 years old on 22 January 1901, after reigning for 63 years.

Pictured: *The house in Nottingham where William Booth was born in 1829.*

Complete this newspaper report:

Nottingham News
1844

Only 2p

17 FOUND DEAD AT GALLOWS

Latest reports from Nottingham confirm that at least seventeen people have died as a result of

_____

_____

_____

_____

_____

_____

_____

_____

_____

Reported by: _____

Which line should William use to catch the fish?

❖ •••••• SEE **TRAVEL WITH WILLIAM BOOTH** PAGE 25–26

On the move and hard times ahead!

The city of Nottingham was becoming very poor. Many stocking-weaving factories were losing money and closing down, and many people who lost their jobs were turning to crime. The sight of families being made homeless, and children wandering the streets hungry, made William very upset—even at an early age. Murder and arson were becoming more common, and William's house even had its railings torn down from the front garden by angry mobs who wanted to use them as weapons! Samuel Booth's business began to have problems, and so the family moved to a Bleasby, about fifteen miles outside Nottingham. Business became better for a while, so William started going to a local village school.

Then, once more, his father's business ran into trouble, and at the age of six William and the family moved back to Nottingham. Business began to pick up again and Samuel enrolled William into a well-known college to continue his education.

William often used to play in the streets before and after school and he often noticed a lady and gentleman who would pass by and stop to watch him play. One day they asked him how he was getting on at school. In those days, having a conversation with someone you did not know was a safe thing to do, and so William and the couple became friends. The strangers explained that he looked just like their own son who had died some years earlier. The friendship grew and William eventually discovered that they went to the local Methodist church and so, with his parent's permission, they occasionally took him with them.

FACT BOX:
The castle in Nottingham was destroyed by the riots in 1831 but was re-opened in 1871 as an art museum.

Pictured: Mary Booth, William's mother.

Match the pairs of stockings

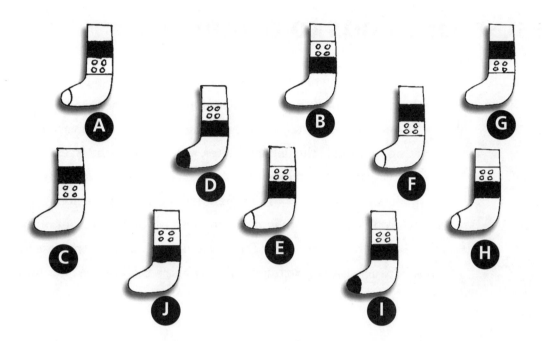

Use the keyboard code to work out the name of William's college:

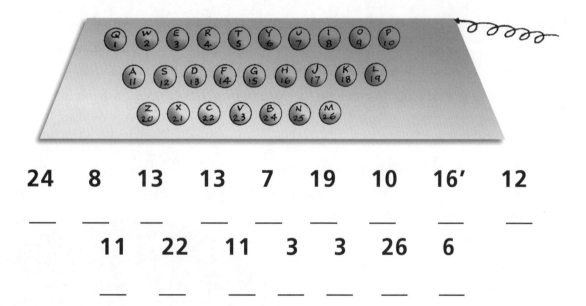

24 8 13 13 7 19 10 16' 12

___

11 22 11 3 3 26 6

___

The start of things to come!

Crime in the towns became worse, and in 1838 a very hard winter caused the River Trent to freeze completely. Many people were homeless due to the loss of so many jobs, and with no homes and little food or shelter, many died in the freezing cold. Army troops patrolled the streets as rumours spread that some people might start to riot. Samuel Booth ran into money problems yet again and was forced to take William out of the academy. He arranged for a local pawnbroker, by the name of Francis Eames, to take William on as a trainee—William was only thirteen years.

In September 1842 William's father, Samuel died. William was sad, but was secretly glad that at least his mother was still alive.

At first William thought his job as pawnbroker was a good way of providing poor people with a chance to gain food and drink by selling the few items they owned. However, he was very upset when he learned that many women were coming in to the shop and selling their wedding dresses or rings, not to buy food for the children, but to provide drink for their alcoholic husbands.

During the first two years of his training at the pawnbrokers, William attended his local parish church, St. Stephen's. He didn't enjoy going, and described the services as 'formal and unfriendly'. He never forgot the Methodist church he used to go to. He liked the idea that the Methodists believed that the way they lived their lives, and the things they did for others, was an important symbol of their Christian faith.

Pictured: The sign of a pawnbroker's shop is still three golden balls.

FACT BOX: PAWNBROKERS

A pawnbroker was a person who ran a shop to buy goods from poor people. It was a way that they could raise money to pay off debts or simply to survive. Later, if they could afford to, the poor people could buy their goods back – but they had to pay interest.

Write the answers to these clues in the grid:

William's age when he left school (8)
The month William's father died (9)
Women needed money to buy this for their husbands (7)
The pawnbroker was called Francis _ _ _ _ _ (5)
What froze over in 1838? (5,5)
Rumours said this might break out (4)
_ _ _ _ troops patrolled the streets (4)
The name of William's father (6)
William worked in this shop (11)
Women were ready to sell this to get money (12)

Three golden balls are the sign of a pawnbroker

What would you sell at the pawnbroker's shop?
Which item below is worth the most if

A=1 B=2 C=3 D=4 E=5 F=6 G=7 H=8 I=9
J=10 K=11 L=12
M=13 N=14 O=15 P=16 Q=17 R=18 S=19 T=20 U=21
V=22 W=23 X=24 Y=25 Z=26

__+__+__+__ =__ __P

__ __ __ __

__+__+__ =__ __P

__ __ __

__+__+__+__+__ =__ __P

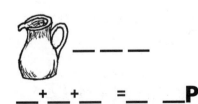
__ __ __
__+__+__ =__ __P

Unsettled times and a pencil case solution!

The Methodist church in William's town could hold up to 2000 people. Imagine this number of people singing hymns on a Sunday morning! This was one of the things that attracted so many—including William.

William hated his work but wanted to become a 'rich young gentleman'. He was a fairly good person, but at the Methodist church he heard that he had done and thought wrong things during his life. He also hated seeing what was happening in the towns and cities around him. William often went to the chapel, and each time he became more unsettled. Sometimes he would go fishing at his favourite spot on the River Trent, just to think about things.

On one occasion, in 1844, he had been given a silver pencil tin by two friends as a thank you present for a favour. Actually Booth had earned money from what he did—but he didn't tell them that! He became worried that he had lied to his two friends, and he felt that he needed to return the pencil tin and be honest. Afterwards, he felt a great sense of peace and now determined to serve God.

Booth's best friend was a young man called Will Sansom who had a strong Christian belief. Both William and Will were keen to help the poor and needy around them. At the age of fifteen, William regularly worked thirteen hours a day in the pawnbrokers shop and then joined with Will to go and make friends with the sick people in the town.

Pictured: *The Methodist chapel that William attended, as it would have been in his time.*

FACT BOX: METHODISM

Methodism started as 'The Holy Club' by a group of students from Oxford University. They were determined to please God by the way they lived their lives, and they believed that they needed a personal relationship with God. John Wesley was their founder.

Symbol	Grid reference	Building
🏛	I1	St .Stephen's Church
🏢	E4	William's first house in Sneinton
⚖	D2	Eames' Pawnbrokers
🏛	B2	Biddulph's Academy
🏠	C4	The Methodist Chapel
🏠	G3	William's home in Bond Street

Use the grid references to draw the symbols on the map in the correct boxes.

Preaching to beggars!

William and Will would pray with the sick people and invite them to sing a hymn. Both boys were as keen to teach people about the Bible as they were to help their physical needs. Will Sansom opened a special mission house in the slum areas of Nottingham and William went along to help him. William was too scared to stand up and preach, but one day he had his first chance to preach about the Bible to a huge crowd in a road called Kid Street. One thing that troubled William was that although there were many sick people in the Methodist meetings, there were never any poor, homeless or jobless people there.

There was a very old lady in Nottingham who was dressed in filthy rags, had no home and used to shuffle about the town, eating whatever she could scavenge and sleeping wherever she could find shelter. Local children teased and laughed at her. She was unhappy and very sick. William and Will and felt sorry for her and set about collecting money. They managed to get a small cabin for her to live in, and provided food for her each day.

William and Will now firmly believed that it was even more important to be forgiven by Jesus for the things people did wrong, than it was for them to be well fed and well clothed. The number of people whose lives were changed by what William taught grew, but some of the local Methodist preachers warned him that things were getting out of hand! This didn't worry William, in fact, it made him think even more about the importance of poor people hearing about Jesus. One day he took action!

Pictured: *Kid Street, where William Booth preached his first sermon in 1846.*

FACT BOX:
It is estimated that John Wesley, the founder of the Methodists, travelled over 250,000 miles (mostly on horseback) and preached 40,000 times during his life!

Help the beggar woman

You will need a friend and dice.
Your task is to collect all the things needed to help the beggar woman.
Take it in turns to throw the dice and tick off each number on the list to collect items. The winner is the first person to collect all the items.
(You have to throw the exact number to collect the item: a one for money, two for cabin and so on.)

Money
1

Cabin
2

Table
3

Chair
4

Bed
5

Food
6

Money
1

Cabin
2

Table
3

Chair
4

Bed
5

Food
6

Beggars can't go to church!

The Methodist chapel was full with well-dressed worshippers, and the preacher was about to begin his sermon. Suddenly, the main doors were thrown open and a crowd of ragged, smelly, dirty and disease-ridden homeless people shuffled in. Behind them was an excited William Booth. William had been into the slums of Nottingham, an area known as 'The Bottoms'. He had been preaching to these people and decided to get them into church—so he brought them! William escorted them to the best seats usually reserved for the regular worshippers. Booth then sat right in the middle of them, feeling very happy and excited.

At the end of the service, William was summoned to meet the church leaders, who were not at all happy! They told him that people like this would only be allowed into the chapel if they entered through the back doors and sat on wooden benches behind a screen—this way, the more sensitive members of the congregation would not be 'put off' and fleas would not get into the cushions! Although not happy with this, William took the 'telling off' well, but deep inside he was sad that the Methodist church had changed its mind from the first message of care that he once heard.

THINK BUBBLE: Do you think William was right to upset the church goers by bringing in these homeless people?

In spite of this, William was invited by Samuel Dunn— one of the church leaders who told him off—to preach at a local village chapel. During this time, he was still working at the pawnbrokers, however this too, was about to change.

Pictured: *It was through this street, much smarter today, that William brought the homeless people into the chapel.*

Match the think bubbles to the right person

Oh, what a smell!

They must hear the gospel

What are THEY doing here?

They should not be allowed in here!

They need to be saved

William Booth

Churchgoers

Attitude check

☞ A new child starts in your class. What would you do?

_____

_____

☞ One of your friends is making fun of the new boy at school.
What would you do?

_____

_____

☞ One of your friends is doing a sponsored walk and has asked you to help.
What do you do?

_____

_____

? ? ? ? ? ? ? ? ? ? ? ? ? ?

⬩⬩⬩⬩⬩⬩⬩ SEE **TRAVEL WITH WILLIAM BOOTH** PAGES 46–47

Unemployed, and a new future?

William was the hardest worker in the pawnbroker's shop and there were so many poor people needing their help that they often worked on Saturday until well past midnight. He was not happy about this because he had strong views about keeping Sunday as a special day to worship God. William spoke to his boss, Mr Eames, about it, but rather than being helpful, he sacked William!

However, Eames soon realised his mistake and asked Booth to come back. He even left him in charge of the business while he went off on holiday!

At the age of nineteen William's apprenticeship came to an end and he now had to make some serious decisions. He had no full-time job, and Samuel Dunn told him to think about becoming a full-time Methodist minister. William was not convinced this was right, and he made the decision to leave Nottingham and go to London where he was convinced he would earn his fortune.

Getting a job in London was not as easy as he thought, and he was forced to do the only job he knew—an assistant pawnbroker! He attended a small Methodist chapel and was soon invited to preach there to what he described as a 'respectable, but dull and lifeless congregation.' It was not long before he took his message onto the streets of London but he missed his family and friends, especially Will Sansom, and was not happy in his job. He began to think about working full-time in his Christian preaching.

FACT BOX:
William lived on the premises of the pawnbrokers shop and described his conditions as being that of a 'white slave'.

Pictured: *Kennington Common, London, opposite the pawnbroker's shop.*

Help William choose the right route to get to London.

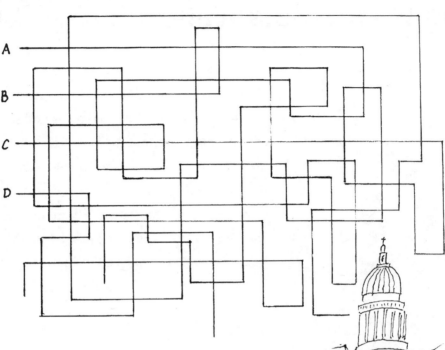

A

B

C

D

Start at the arrow and work around the grid in a clockwise spiral to find out who William worked for in London, and his address. Write your answer in the banner.

London

L	I	A	M	F	I	L
L	O	N	S	O	U	M
I	T	D	O	N	T	E
W	G	N	O	L	H	R
▲▲	N	I	N	N	E	K

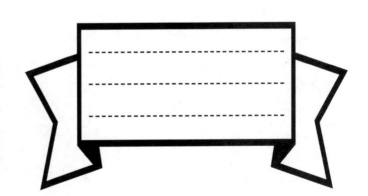

Rearrange
the letters to see how William
was feeling in London

Y E L L O N

— — — — — —

❖•••••• SEE **TRAVEL WITH WILLIAM BOOTH** PAGE 48–53

Rabbits and romance!

A group called 'The Reformers', wanted the Methodists to return to the love for others that they first had. One of these was called Edward Rabbits. He was a rich man, who many thought was a millionaire. He owned a chain of boot-making factories and shops. On one

occasion, Edward Rabbits went to the local Methodist church to hear William preach, and was so impressed that he invited William to his house for a dinner party. During the meal, Mr. Rabbits told William he should consider a full-time job as a preacher. He asked William how much he needed to live on each week. William replied, 'Less than twelve shillings sir.' Mr Rabbits responded, 'Nonsense. You cannot possibly live on less than twenty shillings a week—I will supply this for the first three months.' William was very excited and immediately planned to leave his job as a pawnbroker. He became a full-time missionary on 10 April 1852—his twenty-third birthday, which also happened to be Good Friday!

Mr. Rabbits was very friendly with the Mumford family, and Catherine Mumford was also at that dinner party. Catherine was a great supporter of William and the two of them had a lot in common. A few weeks later, on the day William started his full-time work, Catherine and William met again. This time romance blossomed and he escorted Catherine on her long carriage ride home. On Saturday 15 May 1852, William and Catherine became engaged to be married.

Pictured: *Catherine Mumford, in her early twenties, before she married William Booth.*

FACT BOX:
Missionaries were, and still are, people who give up their full-time jobs in order to spend more time helping others. They also use as much of this time as possible to teach people about the Bible and what being a Christian means. By the way, twelve shillings equals 60 pence in today's money.

Rearrange the columns in order to find out what William thought of Catherine when they first met.

3	1	5	9	12	10	4	2	8	6	11	7
F	I	L	V		E	E		O	L	R	
E		D	D			A	H	N			A
R	E		L	E	O	S	A		I	V	N
W		T	H		E	I		T	H		
		R	O		U	P		I	E	S	C
W		M	W		H	O			A	O	N
E		A	M		Y	C	B		M		E
		W						E	I		F

1	2	3	4	5	6	7	8	9	10	11	12

Rearrange the letters to find out what Catherine had done eight times by the age of twelve

DEAR   HRE   LIBEB

_ _ _ _   _ _ _   _ _ _ _ _

❖•••••• SEE **TRAVEL WITH WILLIAM BOOTH** PAGES 55–57, 65–68

Family life—Booth style!

The Reformers and the Methodists all seemed to be arguing with each other and William felt that they were not properly looking after the new people who came into the church. Then he heard that a little village church in Spalding, Lincolnshire, was looking for a minister. Even though this would mean being away from Catherine, they both felt he should take the job. For eighteen months, William was extremely happy and very successful in this work. He and Catherine wrote to each other all the time. Only on one occasion was there ever a problem between them. Catherine felt that a woman had as much right to preach in a church as a man. William was uncomfortable with this but was too much in love to argue!

William and Catherine were married on 17 June 1855 in South London. They spent a week on honeymoon on the Isle of Wight before sailing to the Channel Islands to hold mission meetings. Some people did not like William's emotional sermons and enthusiastic character. William and Catherine, however, continued travelling around the country holding missions in different churches. Their first child, William Bramwell, was born on 8 March 1856 in Halifax, Yorkshire. By the time their second son, Ballington, was born on 28 July 1857, the family had settled down to a new home and job in a village called Brighouse in Yorkshire.

FACT BOX: Catherine did not much take to sailing and was often very sea sick on these journeys.

Pictured, top: Spalding church where William often used to preach.
Pictured above: William and Catherine seven years after getting married.

Unscramble the place names:

A ____________________

B ____________________

C ____________________

D ____________________

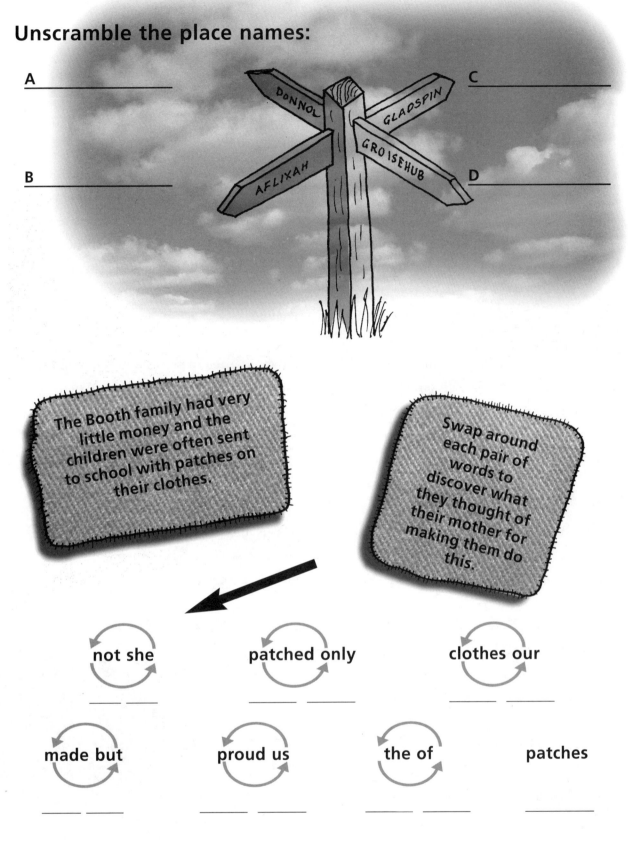

The Booth family had very little money and the children were often sent to school with patches on their clothes.

Swap around each pair of words to discover what they thought of their mother for making them do this.

not she
_____ _____

patched only
_____ _____

clothes our
_____ _____

made but
_____ _____

proud us
_____ _____

the of
_____ _____

patches
_____

ANSWERS:

A. London
B. Halifax
C. Spalding
D. Brighouse

❖•••••• SEE **TRAVEL WITH WILLIAM BOOTH** PAGES 68–75

More homes and more children!

Again the family moved—to Gateshead on the North East coast of England. Three months after arriving, Catherine gave birth to their first daughter, Catherine (Katie). On 8 January 1860, their second daughter, Emma Moss, was born. The Booths worked hard and were even more successful than before. Their church was nick-named 'The Converting Shop', because so many lives were changed (or converted) as a result of William's preaching.

In Gateshead, Catherine felt she wanted to preach, although many were uneasy about this and some even angry. William eventually encouraged her. When William was ill, Catherine took over all his duties as well as her own, and some felt that this was going too far. William was also not happy in a church, as he really wanted to be out in the streets preaching to people. So, he resigned.

With no home, money or job, but with a growing family, the Booth's went to stay with Catherine's parents in London. Soon, William and Catherine were invited to preach in Cornwall. They were excited, and left immediately in August 1861. Again they were successful and stayed until August 1862. Before they left, another boy, Herbert, was born.

The Booths felt they needed to settle down in order to bring up their family. Their sixth child was born, a girl called Marian Billups. Catherine was now more popular in her preaching than William and was getting a lot of invitations to preach in London. This would be the next chapter in their life!

THINK BUBBLE: Was Catherine right to preach? Why do you think this?

Pictured, top: Catherine Booth preaching at the city temple, London.

Pictured, left: The Angel of the North in Gateshead is twenty metres high, weighs 208 tonnes and is fifty-four metres wide (about the same as a jumbo jet).

What did Catherine say the first time she stood up to preach?

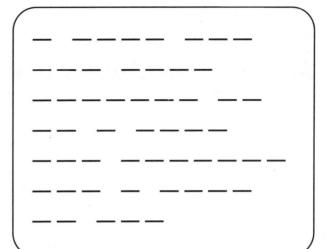

```
l  b  e  o  b  h  r  l  l
h  t  e  t  e  C  i  i  b
a  e  n  g  a  r  s  w  e
v  y  w  n  f  o  t  l  o
e  t  i  i  o  f  .  w  n
n  o  l  l  o  l  N  o  e
```

— ———— ——— ———
——— ———— ——
——————— —— ——
—— — — ——— —
——— —————— ——
——— — ———— —
—— ———

Use the information from pages 2 and 22 to match the dates to the events.

17th June 1855	Ballington born
8th March 1856	Left London for Cornwall
28th July 1857	William and Catherine married
8th January 1860	Left Cornwall
August 1861	Herbert born
26th August 1862	Emma Moss born
August 1862	William Bramwell born

A hard man saves the day

In February 1865, the Booth family returned to Hammersmith in London. Every day Catherine crossed the River Thames to the rough areas where she cared for the poor and sick. William would often preach outside the *Blind Beggar* public house and on many occasions he would return home covered in blood and bruises as not everyone wanted to hear his message.

Peter Monk was a well-known street fighter in the area. William met him and invited Peter to hear him preach. The following evening, after a fight which he easily won, Peter went to the tent where William was speaking. It was packed with rough people who were screaming and shouting, and he couldn't hear what William had to say. So, Peter Monk took off his jacket, rolled up his sleeves, looked menacing, and walked up and down the rows of people. It wasn't long before the whole tent was silent! He believed William's message and was converted.

In November 1865, Catherine gave birth to their seventh and final child, Eveline Cory. The family moved to Hackney. Family life was settled, and although they were very poor, the children were loved greatly. The work continued to grow and was known as 'The Christian Mission'. They hired halls and warehouses, but often had trouble from local youths. On one occasion youths lit a trail of gunpowder leading into the room, and on another they threw fireworks through the open windows. William loved the people and longed to see their lives changed. One milkman used to add water to his milk to save money, but after hearing William preach, he wanted to follow Christ, and he stopped cheating his customers.

> **FACT BOX:**
> **BARE-KNUCKLE PRIZE FIGHTING**
> It was always illegal, but very popular, and often left both winners and losers battered and covered in blood with swollen eyes, broken limbs and knocked out teeth — there were no rules! Soon after Peter Monk's last fight, the Queensberry Rules (1867) were introduced to make it safer.

Pictured: 'The Blind Beggar' in Whitechapel, London. William Booth preached outside this public house in 1865.

**What did William say to Catherine when he saw the masses
of poor people in London?
Start at the arrow and work around the Catherine wheel into the centre.**

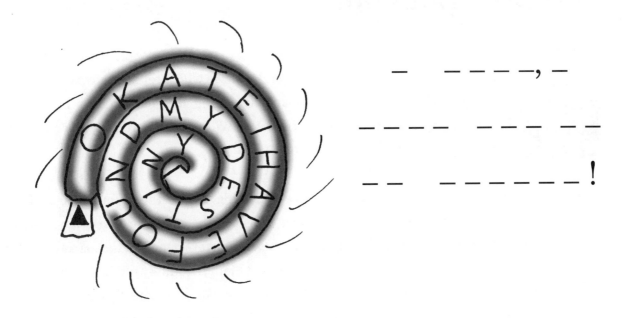

– ––––,–

– – – – – – – – –

– – – – – – – –!

Find 8 differences between the two boxers:

◆••••••• SEE **TRAVEL WITH WILLIAM BOOTH** PAGES 82–84

The work goes on!

A medical student from Ireland became a good friend to William and helped him with his work. His name was Thomas Barnardo who later started the famous Dr Barnardo's children's homes. Also another young man, called Gypsy Smith, brought many travellers from their sites to William's meetings. Gypsy Smith became a well-known preacher too.

The work was growing fast, and William was now preaching all over the country and telling people about his work in London. As well as hiring halls and theatres, the 'Christian Mission' had now turned an old 'beer house' into their first head-quarters. One Christmas day, William had been out preaching to the poor. When he returned to join the family party, he was very worried and declared: 'I shall never spend a Christmas day like this again. The poor have nothing but the public houses!' The next year, 300 Christmas dinners were cooked and delivered to local people in need.

A larger building was bought in 1870 which had once been 'The People's Market'. It was perfect, as it had lots of little kitchens and rooms, and a large main hall that could cope with up to 1500 people. These could be used to prepare the soup and meals that were now being delivered regularly to those in need. A job shop was set up where the unemployed could try to find work, as well as an advice clinic where help was given to pregnant mothers, and to refugees from other countries. William also opened five shops under the name 'Food for the Million', where food was sold as cheaply as possible to those in need.

FACT BOX:
Thomas Barnardo decided to open his first children's home in 1870 after meeting a homeless child called Jim Jarvis. By the time Barnardo died, there were more than 8000 children living in his homes.

Pictured top: *Dr. Thomas Barnardo, 1845–1905.*

Pictured above: *William Booth wanted to see people become Christians, but he also wanted to help them to find food, and homes to live in.*

Who cooked the 300 Christmas dinners for the poor?

Starting with the letter 'C', write down every fourth
letter clockwise around the Christmas dinner plate.

Start letter

Next letter

_ _ _ _ _ _ _ _ _ /_ _ _ /_ _ _

_ _ _ _ /_ _ _ _ _ /_ _ _ _ _

Chunks of bread were sold to the poor for

_ _ _ / _ _ _ _ _

(colour in the dotted shapes to find out)

❖•••••• SEE **TRAVEL WITH WILLIAM BOOTH** PAGES 84–86, 93–100

Elephants, camels and two good friends!

Opposition to the work increased. When a circus arrived where the missionaries normally preached, clods of earth were thrown at them and a brass band played so loudly that no one could hear. Finally, the circus staff led out a huge elephant and two camels—which caused panic amongst the crowds!

William was joined by George Railton and Elijah Cadman. Both were hard working men who were keen to help the work move forward. William and his team saw their work as a battle against sin and that they were soldiers in God's army. In 1877 Elijah Cadman declared 'war' on a small fishing town called Whitby, and he put up posters declaring 'War! War! 200 men and women wanted at once to join the Hallelujah army!' Saying a prayer had the military language of 'knee drill', preaching was called 'bombshells', and collecting an offering of money became known as 'firing a cartridge!'

In May 1878, William wrote a report on his work and he called in his son Bramwell and George Railton to read it. What happened next was the birth of The Salvation Army. Bramwell objected to the words, 'volunteer army', so William wrote instead, 'Salvation Army'.

Following the military theme, each mission station around the country was named a 'corps', a crest and a uniform was designed to identify all members of the army and the motto 'Blood and Fire' was created. A newspaper called *The War Cry* was published. Brass bands were formed to accompany the singing and William insisted that they were to play modern tunes that the poor people would know, so they would be able to join in with the songs.

Pictured: *The Salvation Army Crest. The rays of the sun represent Jesus as the light of the world, and the crown is Jesus as King. Blood was used as a symbol of Jesus dying to take our punishment for the wrong things we do. Fire was used as a picture of the Holy Spirit.*

FACT BOX:
George Railton was a missionary who went to Morocco but ran out of money. He had to work as a Ship's steward to pay for his return to London. He turned up on the Booth's doorstep uninvited and ended up staying for eleven years!

Use the code at the bottom of the page to colour The Salvation Army crest.

Bk=black   Bl=blue   G=grey   R=red   Y=yellow

All the letters in the words and all the points round
the circle are yellow.
If you have it, you may like to compare your finished picture with
that on page 93 of *Travel with William Booth,* or on the image on
the front cover of this book.

A life ends—the work continues

Early in 1888, Catherine Booth was diagnosed with a serious cancer and was given only two years to live. Despite this, William and Catherine felt that the work should continue. The next two years were very difficult. William hated to be away from his wife and yet he found it hard to be with her and watch her die. On Saturday afternoon 4 October 1890, Catherine died. Over the next five days, almost 50,000 people filed past her coffin to pay their respects—that's how loved she was by so many. On 13 October 36,000 people crammed into the Olympia Hall in London to take part in her funeral service.

William threw himself back into the work by publishing a 140,000 word book called *In Darkest England and the Way Out*. It sold 200,000 copies and had a huge impact on the future of the work. Farms were started, employment centres opened, and banks set up to offer poor people loans to buy tools. William travelled the world setting up The Salvation Army in many different countries, including America, South Africa, Australia, New Zealand and India. By 1904 the motor car had been invented and William immediately saw the value in using this to travel the country, particularly as his health was beginning to fail and his eyesight was poor.

William died on 20 August 1912, at the age of eighty-three. The following day the news was announced to the world with a simple message being posted on the door of the international head-quarters: 'The General has laid down his sword'. During sixty years of work, he had travelled five million miles, preached sixty thousand sermons and encouraged sixteen thousand people to serve the 'army' in fifty-eight countries.

Pictured: *This car was known as 'the big white car with red wheels', and was one of the cars that, between 1904–1911, carried the elderly William Booth on missions across the country.*

THINK BUBBLE:
William and Catherine Booth had a huge influence on the world at that time. In what areas would you most like to influence the world? How could you achieve this?

Find these words in the word search.

W	J	K	S	T	S	T	E	P	H	E	N	S	T	I	B	B	A	R	C
L	I	A	M	N	O	E	P	M	R	O	D	O	O	L	B	H	F	A	C
P	G	L	S	A	Y	M	I	L	D	S	T	S	I	D	O	H	T	E	M
P	N	L	L	D	B	W	O	N	O	A	H	G	U	M	N	H	T	S	C
A	A	A	E	I	R	Z	O	S	E	M	A	E	E	P	E	R	S	Q	T
W	F	W	J	H	A	L	K	A	O	Y	C	X	R	R	S	B	N	U	V
N	I	N	L	G	M	M	D	N	C	H	M	G	I	B	W	O	E	N	A
B	D	R	D	N	W	O	B	S	P	L	M	N	T	S	E	P	I	S	Q
R	R	O	R	S	E	T	Y	O	Z	N	E	V	U	L	A	R	N	S	R
O	O	C	V	W	L	U	O	M	O	B	A	L	L	I	N	G	T	O	N
K	F	P	X	B	L	D	K	T	O	H	F	I	F	G	B	O	M	C
E	M	Q	O	N	R	L	T	O	J	I	H	E	D	J	K	C	N	A	A
R	U	R	S	A	M	I	T	N	N	O	T	L	I	A	R	N	O	M	D
S	M	V	N	E	N	H	F	L	K	L	R	S	M	T	U	Q	P	M	M
Z	Y	R	W	G	N	O	T	I	N	T	O	N	E	P	L	A	C	E	A
A	A	X	H	C	M	H	D	A	E	H	S	E	T	A	G	V	W	X	N
B	B	A	D	E	G	I	J	B	L	O	O	D	A	N	D	F	I	R	E
Y	M	R	A	N	O	I	T	A	V	L	A	S	Z	F	S	G	T	E	Y

WILLIAM BOOTH	SNEINTON	NOTTINGHAM
CATHERINE BOOTH	NOTINTONE PLACE	SANSOM
BRAMWELL	ST STEPHENS	RABBITS
BALLINGTON	PAWNBROKERS	SALVATION ARMY
EMMA MOSS	EAMES	CORNWALL
HERBERT	METHODIST	GATESHEAD
BARNARDO	LONDON	RAILTON
BLOOD AND FIRE	MUMFORD	CADMAN

William Booth's Timeline

DATE	AGE	WHAT HAPPENED?
1820		Florence Nightingale was born
1829		William Booth was born at Sneinton, Nottingham
1837	8	Victoria crowned queen
1840	11	Penny post started
1842	13	Father dies and William becomes a pawnbroker
1844	15	William feels guilty about lying to his friends
1849	20	Arrives in London
1851	22	Meets Catherine Mumford
		Crystal Palace built to house the Great Exhibition
1852	23	Starts full-time Christian missionary work in Spalding
1855	26	Marries Catherine Mumford
1856	27	First child, William Bramwell born
1857	28	Second child, Ballington born
1858	29	Third child, Catherine born
1860	31	Fourth child, Emma born
1861	32	Returned to London then worked in Cornwall
1862	33	Fifth child, Herbert born
1864	35	Sixth child, Marian born
1865	36	Final child, Eveline Cory born. Starts Christian Mission in London
1877	48	Alexander Graham Bell invents the telephone
1878	49	Christian Mission becomes The Salvation Army
1879	50	The electric light bulb was invented by Thomas Edison
1880	51	Primary school education made law
1885	56	The first automobile was built by Karl Benz
1888	59	Jack the Ripper terrorises the East End of London
1890	61	Catherine dies
1901	72	Queen Victoria dies at 82 after a 64 year reign
1912	83	William Booth dies

© Day One Publications 2005 First printed 2005

A Catalogue record is held at The British Library   ISBN 1 903087 83 X

Published by Day One Publications Ryelands Road, Leominster, HR6 8NZ

☎ 01568 613 740 FAX 01568 611 473 email—sales@dayone.co.uk www.dayone.co.uk All rights reserved

Series Editor: Brian Edwards

Design and Art Direction: Steve Devane Thanks to Paul Sayer for his invaluable help with the artwork

Printed by Gutenberg Press, Malta